VIEW OF DAWN
IN THE TROPICS

VIEW
OF DAWN
IN
THE TROPICS

G. CABRERA INFANTE

Translated from the Spanish by Suzanne Jill Levine

HARPER & ROW, PUBLISHERS

NEW YORK, HAGERSTOWN
SAN FRANCISCO
LONDON

This work was first published in Spain under the title *Vista del Amanecer en el Trópico.* © 1974: G. Cabrera Infante.

FIRST EDITION

Designed by Sidney Feinberg

Library of Congress Cataloging in Publication Data

Cabrera Infante, Guillermo, 1929–
   View of dawn in the tropics.

   I. Title
PZ4.C1259Vi 1978   [PQ7389.C233]   863   76–5134
ISBN 0–06–010622–0

78 79 80 81 82 10 9 8 7 6 5 4 3 2 1

To the memory of Comandante Plinio Prieto,
  who was shot by firing squad in September 1960

In memory of Comandante Alberto Mora,
  who shot himself in September 1972

Si amanece, nos vamos.
GOYA, *Los Caprichos*

VIEW OF DAWN
IN THE TROPICS

THE ISLANDS CAME OUT OF THE OCEAN as isolated isles, then the keys became mountains and the shallows, valleys. Later the islands joined to form a great island, which soon became green where it wasn't golden or reddish. Islets continued to emerge beside it; now they were keys and the island turned into an archipelago: a long island beside a great round island surrounded by thousands of islets, isles and even other islands. But since the long island had a defined form, it dominated the group, and nobody has seen the archipelago, preferring to call the island "the island" and to forget the thousands of keys, isles, islets, that border it like clots of a long green wound.

There's the island, still coming out between the ocean and the gulf: there it is. . . .

> *. . . history begins with the arrival of the white
> men, whose deeds it records.*
> FERNANDO PORTUONDO

BUT BEFORE THE WHITE MAN WERE THE INDIANS. The
first to arrive—they came, like all of them, from the
continent—were the Ciboneys. Then came the Tainos,
who treated the Ciboneys like servants. The Ciboneys
didn't know how to till the earth or make utensils; they
were still in the gathering stage when the Tainos
arrived. In turn the Tainos and the Ciboneys were
at the mercy of the Caribs, ferocious cannibal war-
riors, who were constantly raiding the eastern part
of the island. The Caribs were fierce and proud
and had a motto: *"Ana carina roto"*—"Only we are
people."

When the white men arrived they marveled at the
sight of the island: "More beautiful than any I have
seen, filled with trees, verdant and luxuriant, all along
the river . . ." Some explorers sent to reconnoiter the
surroundings returned with praises for the hospitality
of the aborigines, many of whom "carry a burning wood
in their hands, with certain herbs to fume," and also
praising "a varietie of birds" and "a great varietie of
trees, herbs and fragrant flowers" and "dogs that do
not bark." The natives went around half naked, both
men and women, and they were very unsuspecting.
They had, besides, the dreadful habit of bathing so
much that when the king was informed, he issued a
royal decree recommending that they not bathe too

much, since "we believe that it could do you much harm."

When the discoverers arrived, there were more than one hundred thousand Indians on the island. A hundred years later there weren't even five thousand: they had been decimated by measles, smallpox, influenza and bad treatment, in addition to suicide, which they began committing in great numbers. On the other hand, there were battles between the Indians, armed only with bows and arrows, and the visitors, who rode armored horses and wore armor, thus becoming truly ironclad machines. The natives, in turn, lavished upon the conquistadores two plagues: the vice of smoking and syphilis, which was endemic among them.

In the beginning the rebel natives had some success, being favored by the rough and familiar terrain. But they were finally overcome by the sword and the horse.

IN THE ENGRAVING YOU CAN SEE THE EXECUTION, or rather the torture, of an Indian chief. He's tied to a stake on the right. Flames are already beginning to cover the straw at the foot of the stake. A Franciscan priest, with his shovel hat hanging down his back, approaches him. He has a book—a missal or a Bible—in one hand and in the other he bears a crucifix. The priest approaches the Indian somewhat fearfully, since a bound Indian is always more frightening than a free Indian—perhaps because he can break loose. He is still trying to convert him to the Christian faith. On the left of the engraving there's a group of conquistadores in iron armor, with muskets in their hands and unsheathed swords, watching the execution. In the center of the engraving is a man meticulously occupied in bringing the torch close to the Indian. The smoke from the blazing fire fills the whole upper right side of the engraving and you can no longer see anything there. But in the background, on the left, you can see several conquistadores on horseback, pursuing a half-naked crowd of Indians who flee rapidly toward the edges of the engraving.

The legend says that the priest came close to the Indian and suggested that he go to heaven. The Indian chief knew little Spanish but understood sufficiently and knew enough to ask: "And the Spaniards, they also go to heaven?" "Yes, my son," said the good father from amid the bitter smoke and the heat. "Good Spaniards also go to heaven," in a paternal and kindly tone. Then the Indian raised his proud chieftain's head, with long, greasy hair tied behind his ears and the aquiline profile still visible on the beer bottle labels that bear his name, and he said calmly, speaking from amid the flames: "Better I not go to heaven, better I go to hell."

UPON REACHING A LARGE VILLAGE, the conquistadores found some two thousand Indians gathered in the central square, awaiting them with gifts—a quantity of fish and also cassava bread—all of them squatting and some smoking. The Indians began to hand out the food, when a soldier took out his sword and attacked one of them, lopping off his head in one stroke. Other soldiers imitated the action of the first and without any provocation began to swing their swords left and right. There was even greater butchery when several soldiers entered a *batey*, a very large house in which over five hundred Indians had gathered, "among whom few had the chance to escape." Father Las Casas tells us: "There was a stream of blood as if many cows had been slaughtered." When an investigation of the bloody incident was ordered, it was found out that the conquistadores, receiving such a friendly reception, "thought that so much courtesy was intended to kill them for sure."

A MAGNIFICENT MACHINE WAS INVENTED to track down and destroy escaped Indians and runaway slaves: the killer bloodhound. Its fame spread throughout the territory and very soon many were exported to the United States' southern regions, where they were known as Cuban hounds.

THE TOBACCO PLANTERS HAD RISEN IN PROTEST against the monopoly decreed by the government. Not all of them were in the uprising, but those who weren't saw their crops destroyed by the mutineers. Now they were a mob of eight or nine hundred men, who threatened to march on the capital. But the alerted captain general sent a troop of two hundred well-armed men to meet the planters. The troops waited in ambush and when the mutineers appeared, they fired upon them, killing many and capturing the rest. Of the wounded, eight died and the eleven of the advance guard who had been captured were executed, without a trial and by order of the captain general, and their corpses hung "from different trees on the main thoroughfares as a public warning."

THE CITY WAS UNDER SIEGE for more than a month and a half. Finally the English managed to dynamite a passage behind the Morro fortress and enter through there. Before the attack, the earl in command of the English forces sent a message to the commander of the fort demanding his surrender. But the commander refused to surrender, announcing that he would fight to the finish. The English troops entered the Morro and found almost no resistance, since most of the defenders surrendered or fled toward the city. During the attack the commander of the fort was mortally wounded, falling with his sword in hand. This show of courage to the enemy was admired by the English, who ordered that he be carried to the city to be tended by physicians. When the commander died, the English joined in the mourning, firing their rifles into the air as a final salute.

IN THE ENGRAVING YOU CAN SEE A BAND OF SLAVES. They are led, four abreast, by one slave driver at the head of the line, and another spurring them on with a whip. The slaves are joined by a clamp, usually made of wood. They are barefoot and half naked, while the slave drivers wear sombreros to protect them from the sun. One of the slave drivers smokes a cigar and doesn't seem to be in a hurry to take his band to its destination, while the other snaps the whip in the air. Behind the group you can see a palm tree and several banana trees, which give the rest of the engraving an exotic, almost bucolic touch.

HISTORY SAYS: "The colored people began to nurture among themselves the goal of imitating the Haitians. The insurrections of the blacks in the sugar mills were more and more frequent, but they lacked unity and leadership."

Legend has it that the largest uprising was crushed in time because the governor himself found out about it when, during his rounds, he heard some blacks talking in a hut outside the town walls.

In reality, as often happens, the conspirators were betrayed by a neighbor who lived in the house on whose roof the conspirators would meet.

All the conspirators were hanged.

HE WAS A POET and the son of a Spanish dancer and a mulatto barber and he had to earn his living as a comb-maker. He had some talent and his poems began to be known and appreciated on the island. But he longed to be known outside.

His life was marked by misfortunes. When he was born they deposited him at the orphanage and when he was barely thirty-five he was apprehended, accused of conspiring against the colonial powers and sentenced to be shot. During the trial, in which they couldn't prove him guilty of any crime, he remained serene. He spent the night before the execution writing a prayer in the form of a poem. With it he achieved posthumous fame abroad.

His life was marked by contradictions. He was born in Venezuela, and still very young, he joined the Spanish army and fought against the liberators of his country. He came to the island with the troops defeated in Venezuela. He wore a colonel's insignia and "was known for his bravery." He was also known as a sportsman and a man about town. He was very good-looking and cut quite a figure in the salons of high society. He finally married a girl from a rich Havana family and was transferred to Spain, then engaged in the Carlist wars. There he was rapidly promoted until he became field marshal. He returned to the island with important commissions. But in some way—perhaps his sporting life was the cause—he began to conspire against the colonial powers of which he was still a part. He had to flee the country.

He returned as the leader of an expedition intended to "free the country from its colonial yoke." The campaign was a failure, but for the first time he fought on the island under the banner that, through the years, would become the national flag. He again fled abroad, escaping almost miraculously. A short while after, he organized another expedition, which also failed. But this time he was caught, tried and sentenced to die on the gallows. They say that he went up on the scaffold smiling to the crowd that came to attend the execution, with the same elegant smile he had displayed in the city's drawing rooms barely ten years before.

HE MARCHED AT THE HEAD OF A COLUMN of "some two hundred men," "very few of whom carried firearms," toward the neighboring town. He assumed he could occupy it without resistance, since there would be no other troops there except some *salvaguardias* from the local vigilante group. "On the way there they made a short stop at the sugar mill . . . and then at the plantation . . . where they had lunch. They continued the journey in the afternoon, thus arriving . . . at nightfall of the aforementioned Sunday the eleventh. . . . As a precaution, the *caudillo* stopped before reaching town and ordered a reconnaissance." He also sent a surrender order to the regional captain, who "offered to surrender at his own discretion."

But at that very moment an enemy column was entering the town from the other side, and when they learned that the rebels were near, they organized an ambush in the square. The rebel column entered the square in darkness, shouting *viva*, and received an unexpected volley of gunfire which forced them to retreat "in complete disorder." But the town became a symbol of the country's fight for freedom.

THE INSURGENTS succeeded in taking an important city and entered it "in the midst of general patriotic intoxication."

The bells of several churches rang at the same time, guns were fired in the air, horses reared, when, "at the request of a fiery crowd," Perucho Figueredo, seated on his horse, composed verses to be sung to the rhythm of a march he had also composed, borrowing from Mozart, which they all hummed. The verses began:

> *To battle run, ye men of Bayamo,*
> *Our fatherland proudly observes thee.*

Barely a century later, jokers sang it with a few changes, like this:

> *To battle? Run, ye men of Bayamo . . .*

THE ENEMY TROOPS, under the command of a count, could boast of nearly three thousand men, while the rebel column had barely five hundred riflemen. The battle—or rather the massacre—took place by a river that is now a dusty ditch. The result of the battle of machetes against cannon fire was not long in doubt. "The army of patriots had to retreat in great disarray, and the Spaniards, taking advantage of that moment, hastily buried their corpses and continued their march toward Bayamo, without finding any obstacle there."

But the rebels decided to burn the city—the first they had taken—before handing it over to the enemy, and when the count entered it he found only ruins, still burning, and ashes, which flew like dust on the windy savanna.

SERIOUSLY WOUNDED, he stayed behind in the rebel hospital. When he got better he knew that he would be a cripple for life. Nevertheless he decided to stay there. "Here I will be useful," he wrote in a letter. When the army moved on to another campaign, he didn't go with them because he had become attached to the region: he liked the strange giant ferns and the classes he'd give to the children in the area, and also his morning excursions to gather wild honeycombs. He also liked to write letters, and every once in a while a courier, whom he taught to read and write, would pass through. "I'm satisfied with what I have," he wrote to his wife. "I live in a hut or in the open air, amid strange arboreous vegetation. I feel strong. I eat what they give me: fruit, and occasionally the meat of yard birds, and hutias, and wild pigs." He was a naïve man and he adorned the mountain with his romantic prose: ". . . the nightingales sing and charm the vesper and from the peaks there descends a fleeting, gallant little brook." Despite the pathetic fallacy and even though his hovel had become a hut and the mockingbirds and thrushes evening's nightingales, he also knew how to look at reality. One of the generals met with a foreign journalist at the village and he served as translator, and somehow the enemy learned of his hiding place. The courier came to warn him, but he calmed him down and all he did was to write letters. "I believe that I will never die a prisoner," he wrote to his brother, "since my gun has six bullets, five for the enemy and one for me. After knowing such freedom, I could never live as a prisoner. Between death and prison, I choose death."

A little boy comes to warn him at dawn that the army is approaching, and he limps out of the village. He hides in the jungle all morning. At noon he feels thirsty and looks for curujuyes, the parasite plant, enemy of the tree and friend of the traveler: they are all dry already. He is on his way down the mountain toward the river, when a wandering sentry spots him. He shoots, wounds the sentry and runs toward the stream. He feels a blow in his leg and knows that they got him. He takes shelter among the great white rocks. A soldier prepares to jump down on him from above, and he shoots him point-blank. The soldier rolls down among the stones; he stands up straight to look at him: it's the first man he's ever killed. And the last: a bullet enters his neck, another his chest, another his stomach. He falls in the water and floats downstream, his body finally resting among the roots.

IN THE ENGRAVING, published in New York, you can see in the foreground four *mambises*—that's what the rebels called their insurgent army to distinguish it from the guerrillas, who were made up of Spaniards or Cuban traitors—three on foot and one on horseback. The rider is black and wears his machete on his belt. Two of the others are also black and, unlike the rider, they're barefoot. One of them is sitting on the right, his head leaning against his rifle. The other black chats with a white *mambí;* he's wearing a kerchief on his head, while all the others wear palm-leaf hats. The white *mambí's* sword is unsheathed and he holds it nonchalantly in his right hand while with his left he takes the reins of the horse, a criollo pony, fourteen hands high. The *mambí* with the pirate-style kerchief on his head sports a rifle with a bayonet. While he chats with the white *mambí,* he holds his rifle in front of him, almost at attention. In the background, to the right, you can see two *mambises,* one white and the other black, talking under a palm tree. Farther to the right there's a banana- or coconut-tree leaf. On the left, in the foreground, there's a tree which seems to be an *ateje.* Way in the background but in the center of the engraving you can see a sentry.

HE WAS A POET TURNED REVOLUTIONARY and he was on several expeditions which ended in shipwreck. Convinced that one should make peace and not make war, he returned to the island with a safe-conduct from the governor general. But when he arrived at the insurgents' general headquarters he didn't say a word. "He didn't make any move at all," the rebel leader later said.

When he returned to the city he was put in prison despite the safe-conduct, and locked up in a cell at the fortress. He was in prison for several months, silently accused of being a traitor by the rebels, and publicly accused by the enemy as a rebel.

Locked in his cell, he wrote this poem:

> *Don't fly, restless swallow,*
> *In search of my dark and secret grave.*
> *Can't you see?*
> *Over the poet's grave*
> *There is no cypress tree, no weeping willow!*

They finally shot him at Foso de los Laureles, which was actually a dry moat.

THE TROOPS CALLED THEIR LEADER THE MAJOR out of respect for his character more than as an acknowledgment of rank. One day the Major was out on horseback inspecting the field, practically alone, when he was struck down by a bullet. Immediately confusion reigned among his men, who tried to rescue his body. But the enemy fire got thicker and they were forced to abandon the quest.

Later, almost by chance, the enemy found his corpse in the tall grass. When they searched him they realized it was the Major and they quickly transported the corpse to the capital of the province, where it was cremated and the ashes scattered to the wind. They did everything so hastily that it seemed as if they were afraid that even his ashes might rise up in revolt.

THERE WEREN'T EVEN TWO DOZEN; they weren't armed: they had only surprise and courage on their side. They carried sticks and stones and their canteens for drinking or storing water, maybe one shotgun. Naturally they didn't take the garrison. But the attack scattered the regiment and they grabbed some rifles and a lot of ammunition.

The invading column took the fort a week later, and the horses, rebels and dead soldiers, whom their sheltered comrades did not dare come out to bury, were still up there, on the plateau. Also, a wounded rebel was up there, who told the story of the attack with tired, hurried words. The colonel couldn't believe it, but he saw the dead men and animals rotting in the sun, and the tin jugs clanking and shining in the night as if they were bayonets and machetes. Then he spoke to the troops and said that he had seen brave, fearless and even crazed men at war, but that these martyrs (pointing to the dead), and the heroes who came out of the battle alive, were the bravest of the brave. Then someone handed him one of the jugs, which had been pierced by a bullet, and the colonel, whose beard and hair prevented them from seeing his face clearly, pushed his hat back. In his voice one could hear his emotion and respect when he said, looking at the jug: "And I called these things impedimenta!"

THE GENERAL HAD SET UP CAMP with a handful of men, when they were caught off guard by the enemy. Ordered to surrender, he decided that suicide was better and he shot himself in the chin. The bullet pierced his mouth and nose and came out at his forehead, where it would soon become a star-shaped scar.

When they informed the general's mother that he had surrendered, she answered that they couldn't mean her son. When they explained that before he was captured by the enemy he had shot himself, she said: "Ah, that's my son, all right!"

THE NEPHEW TALKED ABOUT HIS DEAD UNCLE as if talking about a mythical hero. It's true that his uncle was a living legend. But sometimes it seemed he was exaggerating. Like now. Look, he said, they gave it to 'im in the leg and knocked 'im down and he didn't faint or nothin'—I mean, look, he resisted and kept walkin' with his foot. Of course he hadn't taken more than three steps when he fell right there and then. They got 'im in the knee, see, in this bone here, what's it called, so that one was on top of the other, like that, he said, crossing one arm over the other on his chest, and it wouldn't come down. Then we picked 'im up and took 'im into a hut. The hut was bigger than that there tree, so we hung 'im from the ceiling, see, but his feet still hung down to the floor, he was so tall. Then I got up there and hung 'im by the arms right up there, on the beam, so high up that if I looked down I got dizzy, and then I got down, and hung on to his feet, like this, I grabbed one foot and then the other and I hung there, like this, real hard, by God, with all my strength, and the bone went back into place. And my uncle, he didn't even make a peep and didn't faint or nothin', because I saw 'im sweatin' and I think he saw me sweatin' 'cause it was so hot inside there, all closed in. And what d'you think he said when the bone went back into place and my uncle was still up there on the beam? Hey, he said, nephew, let's see if you can get me down from here—I'm startin' to smell like Christ—just like that, and the God's honest truth, he did look like a crucifix hangin' up there, and as he

33

was a-cursin' and a-swearin' and gettin' into a temper, we took 'im down in a jiffy, just like that, he said, and looked at the gathering, and as he saw some people laughing, he said: I swear by my mother may she rest in peace it's the whole truth, he said, nothin' but the truth. There are people here who know it's so because they were around then, he said. The group laughed again and then the colonel stands up in front of the lantern and says with his pipe in his mouth, chewing the mouthpiece or his words: There's a lot of truth in what he says. That's the way his uncle was, he says. A real man, he said, and they stopped laughing.

THE WARTIME JOURNAL of the nearly bald little man with the big mustache doesn't say what happened at the meeting he and the major general had with the big black general. There has been much conjecture; people have even said that the black general actually slapped the little man in an argument over the military versus the civil command of the insurrection. The fact is that after the war, pious hands tore out the pages of the journal that spoke of the meeting, and thus helped turn the meeting into historic gossip.

The truth is that after the meeting, the little man with the big mustache was elected president of the republic and acclaimed as such by the small regiment.

At that point they asked the black general how the major general could start the invasion with such a small regiment, and the former replied: "He is taking with him a great army: his own strategy."

A few days later the little man, whom they all now called the President, and the major general clashed with an enemy column. No one knows how the incident occurred. Some say that the President saw himself surrounded by enemy forces and tried to evade capture. Others say that the President started running in the direction of the enemy. Still others speak of a runaway horse. The truth is that he received a bullet in his head, falling from his horse very close to the enemy troops, and it was impossible to recover his body. Recognized by the enemy, he was thrown over the back of a mule and the enemy took him with them as the spoils of war. First they buried him in the countryside. But then they exhumed the corpse and embalmed it to take him to the city for burial. In time this corpse became an enormous load on the revolutionary conscience. Converted into a martyr, the little man grew and grew until they finally couldn't stand the weight and all invoked his name, speaking of an immensely great dead man—though when they buried him he was barely five feet five inches tall.

THE DUST FROM THE ROAD (it's July and there's no rain, and the region is a great dust bowl where the slightest breeze raises clouds of white or red or black dirt that erase the roads, camouflage the houses and paint the trees an unhealthy color) made his beard gray. But even before he started to walk with his long, quick martial stride, even before he left his horse, they all knew he was the general. Without saluting, he asked for the other general, who was under his command.

He wasn't coming on an inspection visit or to plan an offensive or even to exchange ideas about the next operation. They would perhaps talk (after chatting about fighting cocks and horses and women, in that order because both of them are peasants, after dessert and coffee at dusk) about the state of the war in general or of the country or they would bet on the days left to the government. He was coming to have lunch, invited to eat a whole cow. A gift from the rancher, said the other general, smiling, when he invited him. Always giving us little gifts; looks like he's a rebel too.

He was late, having avoided enemy posts on the way, and it was already two in the afternoon. The captain told him he would find the other general down by the river, where they done roast the cow (that's the way he said it, using rustic phrasing), and he went down to the riverbank, where bamboo and arum and wild watercress grew, and saw a group by the pit that's still burning. The general has yours, General, said one of them, there under that tamarind tree (pointing). He's been waitin' for ya, he began to say, and stopped when he saw the general's stare.

He walked slowly along the shore, enjoying himself in the fresh air, thanking the river for keeping its bed from the sun and the dust when the streams of the region were dry, saying out loud, Thank you, river, taking off his hat, going down to the water, washing his face and beard and hair, saying thanks again, leaving his head wet, his hair loose and dripping.

The other general was way under the tamarind tree. Eating already, he was living up to his fame, devouring an enormous piece of cow, and the general pretended to be surprised, just a bit. You eatin' that all by yourself? he said, and the other general, with his mouth full of meat, the fat dripping from his chin and hands and arms, a wild joy in his eyes, answered from amid the food: No, sir, the sweet potato's washin' it down. The two of them laughed and the other general pointed to his piece of meat, also big, lying on a royal palm leaf, with green plantains and sweet potato on the side. The general sat down on the grass and began to eat hungrily, voraciously, happy about his first meat in two months. The other general went to the river and took out of the water two brown bottles stoppered with wild cork. He displayed them from afar, one in each hand and up high, like two trout. What luxury, said the general. The bottles were sweating and they drank straight from the cold bottles while they ate and talked and laughed. It was like a picnic.

BUT IT WAS NO PICNIC. Scouts brought the news that the column was already in view. They had to either attack or give up because they lacked a rear guard, and the general decided to attack. The advance guard made contact, they exchanged shots. The bullets buzzed over the rebels and their sound indicated the caliber of the gun, and when to raise their heads.

They were shooting back and forth about ten minutes and the general, tired of the impasse, ordered them to advance. He stood up and went to the edge of the highway. It was a side road, actually a footpath, and on the other side, in the curve, hidden by an embankment, was the enemy. He made the signal to attack and placed himself at the head of the column, as usual.

When they saw him fall, they all believed he had got it in the leg, but the colonel went near him and saw that the general was wounded in the head and in the neck. They also wounded the colonel. Two rebels came and pulled them away from the edge of the road. The doctor crept up on all fours in the crab grass. The colonel had been grazed on the hip, a flesh wound. The general's wounds were fatal. He took a bullet out from under the skin of the skull and said to the third in command that nothing could be done. He pointed to the gray slime that ran down the wounded man's face. A loss of brain matter, he said. He's dying.

They retreated in order, with new casualties. The colonel, bandaged, remained at the head of the troop and ordered that the dead be buried. Then he called the captain and said something to him in a whisper.

They continued the retreat, leaving a rear guard posted.

The burial patrol marched toward three *dagame* trees which could be seen in a nearby stream and the colonel took charge of burying the rebel general and a corporal on the other side of the hill. In a recognizable place, he said, but without identifying the graves. When they left, he walked back and marked twenty paces between the trees. He had remained with two officers and told them to dig. He searched the general, stripping him of his papers, pictures, money, which he kept, and the watch and the gold chain. He took out of his wallet a coin, an amulet, and put it in a pocket of the dead man's combat jacket. He helped them bury the corpse and upon noticing that the dirt on the grave looked fresh, they threw grass and dry leaves and branches on top. Before returning, he made the officers swear that they didn't know where the general was buried, that they had forgotten and that they wouldn't remember it again until the war was over. His identification is a silver dollar on the skeleton, he said.

THEY NICKNAMED THE BIG BLACK GENERAL "Thunder-bolt" and his military feats erased the memory of his clash with the now defunct little man with the big mustache. Whenever the general would lead a machete charge, he'd say to the soldiers: "Who's not with me?" He had risen to the rank of major general before the age of thirty-three and his men, whom he led in the invasion, worshiped him. He was famous for having twenty-two war scars on his body, but he never showed them off. At the peak of his military glory, he displayed even greater courage when he wrote a letter which many considered his political testament: "I have the feeling," he wrote, "that many people want to make me president as soon as we win our independence and I would never consent to that, because most of the people would not look kindly upon such a resolution, for reasons which are better left unsaid in moments like these." Those reasons were, of course, that the general was black. He finished his letter with a personal remark: "From now on, I'd rather think about the trip I'm going to take with my aides, to avoid trouble and disturbances in my free country." That trip was an old wish: the big black general wanted to see Paris, and more than once, in order to keep up the spirits of his war-weary aides, he'd speak to them about La Ville Lumière.

THE OLD GENERAL WITH THE STAR ON HIS FOREHEAD was sitting in his hammock under a *guásima* and a carob tree, dictating a letter. He was informing their delegate in New York about the war, and ended with a comment on the fact that the troops had nothing to do, now that the enemy was retreating and almost the whole province was under rebel command. "We've become fat cats," he dictated, "and if this continues I'm coming over there to work with you, since there's more danger on Broadway than there is here." The aide-de-camp, who was taking down the letter, asked how to spell Broadway.

THE BLACK GENERAL NEVER GOT TO SEE PARIS. In a brief clash, which seemed more like a skirmish, he was wounded to death. He had just turned around to his aide-de-camp to tell him, "This is going well!" when a bullet knocked him off his horse.

The enemy noticed the panic that arose among the *mambí* troops, without knowing why, and thickened its fire upon the confused rebels, killing or wounding several who attempted to recover the corpse.

As the rebels retreated, the enemy raked the area until they found the body of the black general. They searched and emptied his pockets, as they always did, without realizing whom they had killed.

It was not until sunset that a rebel band could come and retrieve the half-naked corpse. Beside the general lay his aide-de-camp, who, incidentally, was the son of the commander in chief.

Before launching the invasion, the Americans sent a message to the general with the star on his forehead, who had promised to give them support.

The day before the landing, the general with the star on his forehead met with two American generals, to agree on their strategy against their common enemy.

The Cuban troops were transported in American warships to participate in the first and only battle the invaders fought. "On the day of the landing," says an enemy historian, "it [the city] was deprived of all the resources it normally received from its farm regions, and a famine resulted; communications were cut off; forests, avenues and hills were all covered with Cubans."

Finally, after a short and almost ridiculous naval battle, the city surrendered to the enemy, which in this case were the friends.

THE OLD COMMANDER IN CHIEF entered the capital with his right hand dislocated and in a sling—as one president would say in the future, "a casualty of popularity," so many times had it been shaken by the multitudes who crowded around him as he passed.

His entry into the capital was a moment of glory and the old commander in chief couldn't get over his amazement, remarking: "Good God, if we had succeeded in having as many troops as admirers, we would have finished off the Spaniards at the drop of a hat," and he added: "Goddamn it, at the drop of a hat!"

IT'S A RADIANT DAY. The sun is shining intensely up above and the transparent air flutters the flag, just hoisted for the first time. Ambassadors and plenipotentiary ministers have gathered on the platform. The newly inaugurated president is also there. Generals and colonels have congregated around the flagpole as well. They have just lowered the Stars and Stripes and the flag with the solitary star is flying out in the open. The day is not only radiant but also auspicious—but this cannot be seen in the photograph.

ALREADY IN THE INDEPENDENCE ERA, the general with the legendary name (known for his manner of capturing, interrogating and exterminating *guerrilleros* by saying: "Tell me what your name is," and then, after the prisoner's answer, adding an ominous ". . . was his name") rebelled against the government in a little war that lasted a few days. But it cost him his life. They found him at dawn, still asleep, and with a machete sliced his head off and sent it to the capital. Years after, they erected a grotesque statue of him in a square in the capital. This time he had his head on his shoulders.

THE HAITIAN AND JAMAICAN WORKERS sent a delegation to speak with the plantation owner. They had decided to end the strike if they received the salary increase. All seemed to be going perfectly well and the owner suggested that they take a picture of the group to commemorate the agreement. The Haitian and Jamaican delegates posed in a row in front of the machine, which was covered by a black cloth. The owner left the group to give an order to his foreman. The foreman uncovered the machine and calmly machine-gunned the group of delegates. There were no more complaints from the sugar-cane workers during that harvest and for many to come.

The story could be real or false. But the times made it believable.

THEY DUG A TUNNEL under the street from the little house to the cemetery. They continued digging to the private mausoleum—it was more a mausoleum than a tomb—making their way through bones and rotting coffins. They dug incessantly to reach the private mausoleum before the funeral. They continued digging through the mud and the carrion flesh and they say that one of the diggers lost his mind. They continued digging until after the assassination, and the same day that the illustrious dead man's funeral was to take place they installed the dynamite and extended the wires through the tunnel and to the house. They were ready by the time of the burial, but the burial didn't take place, and everything—the assassination, the tunnel, the dynamite—turned out to be a waste because the illustrious dead man's family decided to bury him in his native city and not in the family mausoleum. They were able to recover the dynamite, but it was impossible to refill the tunnel and they left the wires, which were discovered by a gravedigger a few days later, while he was digging.

Two others hid on the outskirts of the town. It was very early, but some neighbor saw them or they asked if they could go into another house first. What's certain is that they began searching the houses and someone told them that there were people hiding there (pointing). They looked and didn't find anything. And they were going when someone on the street told them that they did see people go in, that they didn't know whether or not they were the ones from the assault, but that they saw them. They went back to the house and found one coming out of a water tank in the patio. He had been inside it all the time. Two soldiers made him get back in. They kept him under the water at gunpoint and each time he came out they made him go down again. If the head came up out of an instinct of preservation or a reflex or the laws of hydraulics, they pushed it down with their rifle butts. Until he drowned. Then they took him out and threw him onto the patio as if they had just caught a useless fish, a bulk from the sea, a thing.

The other was hidden in the hollow of the A-frame roof, but they saw him now. They began telling him to come down; he started running along the tiles, he ran along the rain gutter, bending down as he crossed the ridge of the roof. He didn't hear or didn't want to hear the orders to stop. He ran faster, perhaps pushed by the decline of the upper slope. He reached the eaves, stopped, put one foot on the drainpipe. He felt it give way. He saw that on the other side was only the corner of the building and the street. He ran—

again in the direction of the patio. He was running slowly, with difficulty, up the roof when one of the soldiers said: Leave it, Sergeant, don't shout anymore— I'll get him down. When the sergeant looked sternly at the soldier, saying: I don't want anybody to go up, the soldier said: I said that I'd get him down, not that I'd go up. The sergeant remained silent, and he was still running up the roof when the soldier took aim and fired.

SHE WAS DOING THE WASH ON THE PATIO when they brought her the news. She didn't say anything or cry or show any emotion. She simply asked: Is it true? The man, the one who spoke, because there were three of them, said yes with his head and explained. They mentioned his name on the radio along with two companions who had fallen. He had his hat in his hand and now he slapped his leg with it. We know that the official report was false, he said. All that about a battle and killed in action is a shameless lie, of course. It was from another source that we learned how it happened. They arrested them and took them to headquarters and killed them there, he said. Then they invented the skirmish. She looked at them and didn't say anything. She was forty, maybe younger, but she looked like an old woman. She wore a tattered dress with little purple flowers and her hair gathered in a bun. Her eyes were a very pale yellow-green and it seemed as if the midday light bothered her. In the silence one could hear the wind between the trees in the patio and a hen cackling. You'll excuse me, she said, but I have to do the wash.

She finished and went into the house and made coffee. She drank it standing, in the doorway, watching how the air became visible between the sheets.

THE CROWD CAME OUT TO CELEBRATE the fall of the dictator. But it was a false alarm. The demonstrators who marched toward the presidential palace were stopped by a machine gun stationed at the palace entrance. Many managed to hide in the fountain in the middle of the park. Others ran to hide behind the trees. And others did an about-face and tried to run away. These suffered the most casualties, killed by the flashing machine-gun fire. There are those who say that the false news of his flight had been circulated by the tyrant himself, a few days before he really had to abdicate.

THE PHOTOGRAPH IS CURIOUSLY SYMBOLIC. It signals the end of a military tyranny at the same time it glorifies a soldier. All the points of the picture converge toward the soldier, who is standing on top of the statue of a lion at the beginning of an avenue in the capital. The soldier is erect, his rifle raised in his right hand, while his left stretches toward one side, perhaps to aid his balance. His head is held high and proud, celebrating the moment of triumph, which is, apparently, collective.

At the extreme left-hand side of the picture, one of the demonstrators has taken off his boater and salutes upward, toward the soldier. To the right and in the center, another, more modest demonstrator (in shirt-sleeves) takes off his cap while he cheers the soldier. They are all surrounded by a small mob, excited by the triumph of its cause, it seems.

Behind the soldier you can see some wrought-iron balconies and some windows with their French shutters wide open. Farther away, in the corner, there's an advertisement for an airlines company, in English. The photograph has been reproduced all over as a testimony to its era—or rather of its moment.

WHEN THEY RAN OUT OF AMMUNITION they decided to surrender. There was a corpse in the garden, beside the bougainvillaea hedge. They couldn't recognize the person when they passed because he had fallen face down. He was wearing a yellow pullover and the man who came down from the porch onto the path wondered who had been wearing a yellow pullover that day. He could glimpse, beyond the gate and on the sidewalk, another dead civilian. But he didn't try to guess who it could be, because he no longer thought about the dead, only about the tanks and soldiers and police outside. Like the others, he was unarmed. Now he saw, out on the sidewalk, the first man to come out of the house, carrying the wounded child, and he saw them arrest him. He and the pregnant woman passed under the iron sign that said Villa Carmita, and as he thought she was slipping and falling, he went to help her. The two fell together, because the first shot knocked them down. On the ground, he was trying to lift the woman, who was dead, when on his white guayabera shirt several red stains appeared, and pushed by the impact he recoiled and landed against the wall. He was dead, but the bullets continued entering his body. One of the columns in the garden was splintered and the sand and brick splattered about.

IT WAS A STRATEGY invented in Chicago during the thirties but perfected here. One car comes first and sprays the marked house with bullets. The occupants or residents come out on the street, frightened and angered, and begin to shoot at the fleeing car. Precisely at that moment another automobile comes by at top speed and shoots at them, wounding and killing a good many. In this instance the technique was being used in a very unorthodox manner. The one who was supposed to die was chatting at the entrance of a movie theater, some say with a friend, while others say the friend was a decoy. In any case, the fact is that one car sped by, spraying the entrance of the theater, shooting haphazardly, without aiming. The one who was to die managed to hide behind a parked car. When the shooting was over he came out of his hiding place, and before he reached the vestibule the bullets got him; this time they were fired by two men on foot. The two gunmen quickly but calmly walked away. The friend (or decoy) had remained under an automobile. The one who was to die died, as one writer described it, with only thirty-five cents in his pocket.

THE AMBITIOUS GENERAL appears, surrounded by army officers, but he's dressed in civilian clothes. This is his third coup d'état in twenty years and he looks smugly satisfied with his power. The general, who likes symbols, is wearing a leather jacket: the same one he wore previously on similar occasions. Later he will swear that in his jacket pocket he always carried a pistol with "one bullet in the chamber"—to kill or to die if his coup d'état failed. But he risked very little, with the commander of the army caught sleeping in his long johns. The general is in the middle of the photograph, with a caption that says: "He is The Man!" That *ecce homo* is meant to be flattering. The general, in civilian clothes, is smiling, perhaps thinking of the historical forces he has just unleashed, but it doesn't show. Around him are colonels and captains who will soon be, in barely a few hours, generals and brigadiers. This strong-armed promotion will divide the island in two. But that doesn't seem to matter to the men in the picture.

incredible, unique free spectacle which interested no one.

Life, friend, is like that dead cow, he said when he finished playing and crossed his hands over the guitar, covering it. See the dead cow: nobody can make you go back, he said to the boy, nor can the jeep go in reverse nor the post office clock slow down, 'cause none of that ain't goin' to save the cow. So the best thing is for each to go his own way: the cow to the slaughter so's the butcher can complete what you guys began, he said, looking toward the boy, who was a recruit, but also toward the corporal and the other soldier in the jeep, who got out at the young driver's insistence to make excuses for the run-over cow. Where were you guys going in such a hurry, you people here go home and go on doing what you were doing, he said, looking toward the regretful farmer behind him, back home to your dead season's misery, and me, I'm going to keep playing until the invisible machine one day, without a sound, catches up with me and my guitar. . . . One of those songs or speeches of yours ought to get stuck in your throat like a sweet potato without butter and choke you, you hear me, said the corporal, staring at him. You never know, Corporal, the black man said. You never know. It's like I say: in life, anything can happen. The corporal noisily planted his boot on the wooden floor of the town's grocery–post office–mayor's office–bar–social club–veteran's center and he shook one hand, pointing a twisted forefinger at the musician. Listen to what I'm telling you, he said, you damn nigger. Black man, the black man said. No, not black man, damn nigger, said the threatening corporal. Just like you say, Corporal; you're the law and God's work and the corporal, said the black man without moving a finger from the guitar, without moving backward or forward, without taking his eyes off the corporal or the three soldiers. Well, said the corporal, you're a damn nigger and a big-mouth and we've got a file on you. So you take your music elsewhere. When we come back, I don't want to see you around here. Take my advice. Remember the cow. I won't forget the cow, Corporal, the black man said. Thanks for the advice. Take his word for it, boy, said the other soldier. Remember the cow, repeated the corporal, moving his finger. Let's go, Corporal, said the boy, the driver, the recruit, please, because if not we'll still be on the road when night comes. What? You afraid? No, Corporal, not afraid, but we don't have lights: the cow made a mess of our headlights. The cow? Not the cow—you knocked into her. I followed your orders, Corporal, said the boy. Yes, I told you to run but not to crash, said the corporal, period, and he turned back to the black man: Remember, I don't want to see you or your guitar or your songs, not even a peep, when I come back, you hear me. The black man said: Just like you say, Corporal.

They left. Before the jeep even started, after being inspected again, and the sun was already hiding, in the indifference of those on the porch looking only at the soldiers, the black man slipped a casual hand over the strings, which sounded what seemed like a chord but was actually the final point of the incident. And when they really left, when they went past the protective curve and beyond the last house of town, the black man played again and sang again and again laughed as he had played, sung and laughed before the soldiers came, when they killed the cow, when they got out of the jeep still stunned by the blow or the surprise, when they looked for the owner and found

THE NIGHT BEFORE, around 2 A.M., the one who seemed to be the leader came in to tell them that they were going to attack the garrison. He didn't tell them which garrison. He said that those who weren't in favor could refuse to join. He would only ask them to stay at the farm for at least two hours after the others left. It would be a security measure for those who weren't going as much as for those who were. One of the men spoke. He was not in favor of the attack. He didn't even know why he was there. He had come with some friends to the carnival. He thought the attack would fail. Nevertheless, he added, I'll go. Two others decided not to go. It's curious. The man who went on the attack without being in favor of it fought, behaved perfectly, and was wounded, but his life was spared. Of the seven who remained in the house, not one survived. The police, the army, the secret service, or whatever it was, discovered the place, surrounded the dwelling and made them come out, shouting at them with a loudspeaker to surrender. They killed them as they came out, one by one.

THERE'S A POPULAR SAYING that when a black man has gray hairs it's because he's old and free of cares. This black man, this man, was old, but walked nimbly and fearlessly down the street although not far off you could still hear occasional shots and from time to time a burst of machine-gun fire, clear, distinctly s-t-a-c-c-a-t-o among the usual sounds of dawn: crowing roosters, birds twittering in the trees, a window opening and a gate banging against an iron railing. He went up Caridad Street with the bread under his arm and greeted someone who passed by. He turned on Espinosa and upon reaching Sebastian Castro and Saldaña streets he heard the engine. He saw the jeep's headlights, still on, appear, and then the whole vehicle, coming over the top of the hill, and he also saw the soldiers. The jeep passed alongside him; he kept on going. Then he heard someone, from behind, calling his name. He turned around and received the shots in his chest, neck and head.

Of course they knew him; everybody in the city knew him: he was a revolutionary years ago and had been in prison and escaped death many times. But not this time. He had been sick a week and since he lived alone, had to go out to buy his breakfast. Everybody knew him and he was lying on the street, dead, with the bread over the pool of blood, until noon or later. He was left lying there as an example, or rather a symbol, of the times when it was his turn to die—which were, like those of all men, bad times to live in.

THE ONLY THING ALIVE IS THE HAND. In any case, the hand seems alive leaning on the wall. One can't see the arm and perhaps the hand is dead too. Perhaps it's the hand of an eyewitness and the spot on the wall is its shadow and other shadows as well. Below, half a yard below, the lawn is burnt by the July sun. There are bare spots in the grass, from footsteps or dirt or cement paths. Now the paths seem bleached, shiny, from the sunlight. A nearby object—a grenade, the shell of a high-caliber cannon, a movie camera?—looks black, like a hole in the photograph. On the path, all over the lawn, there are four—no: five—plain pinewood boxes. (There seem to be six, but that last coffin is the shadow of the wall.) One of the boxes is half opened and there's a corpse in it and in the nearest box there's another corpse, its arm hanging out, as if beckoning the lid. The most visible box, on the right, is nailed and ready for its journey. In the middle of the courtyard there's a solitary corpse, who doesn't have a coffin but awaits one, bent awkwardly, with a garbage can over his head, placed there out of compassion or perhaps mockery. Some trees in the background project a dark shadow. Above, to the left, a wrought-iron hook blends in with the dark trees and looks like a sign. It is only a decoration on the wall or the balcony of the barracks.

ALL THAT'S LEFT OF HIM is a photograph and the memory.

In the picture he's sitting on the floor and looks at the photographer as he will look at death, serenely. He is wounded; you can see blood flowing down his right leg and a dark stain (the wound) on his thigh—and it's not from a bull's horn. So nobody is running to carry the bullfighter to the infirmary. This is not a bullfight and the floor of Moorish glazed tiles is not that of a chapel in a small-town bullring. It's army headquarters, during carnival, on a Sunday. The wounded man did not put on a bullfighter's outfit, because he's not a bullfighter nor did he wish to pose as a matador. He tried to put an end to tyranny and dressed up as a soldier at dawn and came to attack the barracks with ninety other boys. Now the attack has failed and he is lying there on the floor of the guard post waiting to be interrogated. He's not afraid nor does he feel pain, but he's not bragging or even thinking of pain or fear: he is coming to his end with the same simplicity with which he began, and he waits.

Memory knows that seconds later they made him stand up, pushed him around, knocked the cigarette out of his mouth and cursed at him. The photographer gave him the cigarette, the very same man who naïvely thought he could save him with the photograph. They shouted questions at him and he calmly answered that he didn't know anything and couldn't say anything: You are the authorities, not me. They say that only once did he try to touch his wound with his hand, but couldn't, and even though he made no grimace you could see that it hurt like hell. Later they shoved him out, beating him with their gun butts, and when he was limping down the three steps that led to the court-yard they shot him in the back of the head. His hands were still tied, as they are in the photograph.

THEY MADE THEM LINE UP in the prison courtyard. There were five or six, all political prisoners. It was December 24, and an interrogation at night, out in the cold open air, is no Christmas Eve. It was all dark around the prison and you could hear the wind whipping over the roof. Two searchlights were focused on them. Soldiers and not the usual guards were the watchmen. The interrogator, dressed in a colonel's uniform, asked something, first in a low voice, and then he shouted curses at them for several minutes, exhausting his vocabulary of curse words, repeating them, and beginning again, he would again talk quietly, as if chatting.

Then a lieutenant, who always remained in the shadows, put a pistol behind their ears one by one. The colonel shouted each time: Are you going to talk, sonofabitch, are you going to talk! and between the end of his shout and the gunshot you could hear the silence or the wind.

They had been prisoners for days and none could answer the questions about an armed attack made that morning. Before dying, did the last hostage think he was dreaming?

LIKE MANY CUBANS, he enjoyed making jokes about sexual perversions, and his specialty was the perfect imitation of a faggot. A thin, small mulatto, he'd comb his hair with a hot comb and make an impeccable duck-tail. At first when he joined the group, they gave him a certain nickname; but then he revealed that he was brave and cool-headed and daring enough to choose his own alias. He must have been a dancer formerly because he did the rhumba really well, but now he was a terrorist and soon he became the provincial organizer of terrorist action and sabotage, which was a post not everybody could aspire to. Political terrorism is not, what you might call, child's play. And if it's play, it must be similar to Russian roulette.

One of this terrorist's favorite devices was to fasten dynamite securely at his waist, light the wick under his jacket, and then let the stick roll down inside his pants, while he calmly strolled along. A little after he had perfected the technique into a method, he was caught.

Walking up the steps of the precinct, handcuffed to a policeman, he was wondering how he would escape torture, when he thought up a trick. It might work. He was dressed, as always, in jeans with his shirt hanging out and white sneakers, and he walked up the last steps gaily, with almost winged feet, wiggling his hips. As he went in, he smoothed his hair with his free hand, shaping his curl at the same time. The policemen looked at him in surprise. When the sergeant on duty asked him his name and address, he gave in a singsong voice a false name and a false address and an occupation that was also false: exterior decorator. Those who arrested him insisted that he be marked down as dangerous and the sergeant looked him up and down again. This meant that he had to be seen by the head of the precinct. The policemen vouched that he was the head of a terrorist organization and at their insistence the boss came out. Upon hearing the door open and the military steps and seeing the respectful attention with which everyone saluted, he turned around with a gesture that Nijinsky would have found graceful, and swinging only his hips, he confronted his nemesis and the bodyguards with an almost erotic smile. It was a colonel who had begun his career at the same time as the terrorist, but in another direction. The two men looked at each other and the terrorist humbly lowered his long eyelashes. The colonel burst out in a hearty laugh and shouted amid the general laughter: Goddamn it, how many times do I have to tell you to leave the fags alone! Nobody protested; who would dare? They let him go and he went out thanking them in a florid, languid lisp.

But the story has another ending. Two or three months later they caught him again, this time with a carful of weapons. The colonel wanted to interrogate him personally and when he greeted him he reminded the terrorist of their previous interview. He was found a week later in the gutter. They had cut off his tongue and stuck it in his anus.

THE SIERRA IS NOT A LANDSCAPE; it's a scenic back-drop. Before you reach it there is the red and yellow savanna, with torrential rivers or dry riverbeds or end-less grass, or yellow burnt hay or great clouds of dust, depending on the season and weather. And there are the sugar mills, the farms, the cattle ranches: sugar cane and fruit trees and cattle by the thousands. On the other side (one hundred and fifty miles away) is the sea, in waves which sculpt the rocks into abstract coral statues or pebbles or narrow beaches, and (some-times just with the tide) the mountains plunge down into the ocean. Or there are the mangroves, the swamp: inlets of mire and mosquitoes. On the mountain ranges there's tropical vegetation and maybe coconut and palm trees. There is also the jungle growing at night over the path cleared that morning. Sometimes there are bread trees and *curujey* parasite plants among the branches of the ceiba and the *dagame* trees, to aid the traveler dying of thirst or hunger, and as pretty decorations he has the wild orchids. Perhaps he'll find purple star apples or a stray mango or wild papayas and surely sweet custard apples and guavas and trees of rare wood, if the nomadic firewood merchant didn't get there first. Farther up there are no more fruit trees and he begins to find giant ferns and the cork palm and other plants that were there before the deluge. But the jungle is still with him: it's a world of vegetation, though it's possible that he'll see Cuban boas, which are harmless to man. He will also see the hutia, that enormous edible rat, and many, many birds. He'll probably find the strange spectacle of a dead tree blossoming turkey buzzards. Or perhaps another tree with a nest of caracaras on the point of falling because of the weight. He'll see hummingbirds that look like insects, and butterflies the size of birds. His path will now be blocked by the *tibisí* plant, which replaces the *marabú* and the thorn bushes as vegetal dikes, which the machete barely scratches. Here and there he will see a tubular tree trunk a yard or two in diameter: it's the barrel tree, which on the bottom is like a savanna bush and on the top is a perfect living barrel.

The air becomes thin and sometimes the traveler is surrounded by clouds and when they're like a rug it's because there's a precipice below. One walks between abysses along passages a half-meter wide, and one thousand five hundred, one thousand eight hundred, two thousand meters high. The slopes are vertical and the only points of support for your foot or hand are roots and bushes and some hard stone. When you reach a plateau, everything is green: even the sunlight is green. The ground is covered with a herbaceous green carpet; the trees, bushes and jungle run the whole gamut of green. Tree trunks are covered with a lichen that is like green rust and wet to the touch: that green reality is moist. Thousands of pearls of rain drip from the leaves, and as you step, the grass sinks with a crackling watery sound. On the mossy rocks there are crystals of liquid and your path is crossed with tiny streams, veins of water. The temperature is a few degrees above freezing and light barely penetrates the foliage. In a clearing there's a rag of a cloud and the sun pierces it and along the rays climbs a spiral of vapor. There's no breeze, but once in a while you feel a cold gust of wind. Far below is the gray sea on one side, and on the other the savanna now looks gray.

THE DAY THEY CAME THE WAR WAS GOING BADLY. They appeared without warning, like paratroopers. The sentry rejected them, telling them they couldn't stay and that they should go back where they'd come from. They didn't want to, and an officer had to be brought over and they didn't go then either. The camp wasn't very large and the noise reached the head comandante's quarters and the comandante came out. He saw the group, came over to discover what was happening and found the soldiers in an argument with an average-looking farmer and a guy who was so small that he made the other look like a giant. What's going on here? the comandante asked. These guys, who came without weapons and don't want to go back, answered the guard. Is that right? the comandante asked. Yes, said the little guy, and when he stood next to the comandante, who's six foot two, he became a dwarf. The commander looked him up and down, but the other in turn looked him up and down, and they didn't say anything. The comandante smoked his perpetual cigar, moved it from one side of his mouth to the other and exhaled thick smoke, which the small visitor perceived as clouds. They looked like Saint George and the Dragon of the lithographs and they soon would be David and Goliath. No weapons, eh, said the comandante without asking. You can't stay here without weapons, he said, raising his voice. Go back where you came from. We don't have weapons, or food either, he said, and we're not going to be feeding idle mouths. The midget looked at him once more; he seemed to stand on tiptoe, prepare his sling and throw the stone: So if you didn't have weapons, how come you called the people to come fight?

Now the comandante was the one who was disarmed and he could only answer: Okay, Captain, let them stay. But if in the first skirmish, he said, they don't get even only one shotgun, shoot them for me, 'cause we already have enough dead weight, what with our impedimenta, to be carrying around live weights as well. The two newcomers stayed, although they never knew if the comandante had been joking or not. In the next battle the bigger guy didn't pick up any enemy weapon and didn't return to camp. The midget, however, captured a Springfield which was larger than he. Then he fought so much and so well that he soon became a captain and when he died, three days before the war was over, they made him a comandante posthumously.

HE PRETENDED TO MEET HIM BY CHANCE and greet him as you greet an old friend you haven't seen for some time. The other was having beer and he also ordered beer. When the waiter brought the two beers and left, the man who had just got there said to the other man, in a whisper: "The bird's in the cage." The first one, who had already been at the café—that thirty-year-old man who looks forty because of his premature bald spot and the black shadow of his beard and the heavy mustache, but also because of the bitter expression in his eyes, at the corners of his lips, in his mouth when he speaks, an expression like the wake of an old suffering—almost smiling, says, "So he finally came. Great, that's great." He was truly smiling now. "It's all over today," he said.

They asked for another beer and silently toasted success, in what was not precisely a business deal. It was past eleven in the morning and they were still sitting out in the open, watching the clear end of the winter day curve upward into a cloudless sky over the calm blue sea, and their eyes followed the cars rushing by along the avenue. A tall blond girl crossed the street, beautiful and perhaps a bit fat, but Rubens wouldn't think so—nor did the first man, who looked her up and down and threw her a compliment as she passed. After a while another woman crossed: a thin, almond-eyed mulatto, moving her hips as she walked. He threw her a compliment too. The other man, who was shy, smiled at his companion's exclamations of flattery and sipped a little beer. Many women passed the sidewalk café and he always offered each words of praise, talking in his comical Spanish accent. The other seemed to watch him in amusement, but deep down in admiration of a man who in two or three hours would lead an attack on the presidential palace, the most difficult of the commando operations, and would perhaps be dead (and he would), who now seemed a superficial, frivolous and peaceful citizen: a content bureaucrat having his midday *apéritif.*

IF A SERIES OF ADVERSE CIRCUMSTANCES can be called Destiny, then the attack on the presidential palace was destined to failure, as it was written that the ambitious sergeant who rose to the rank of colonel, who pinned the general's stars on himself, who became dictator, would die in his bed of natural causes. Now, they should relive what has already been written, reconstruct history. The vehicles that were transporting the attackers got lost in the afternoon traffic and only two of them reached the back door of the palace on time (the front door was opened only for memorable occasions: ambassadors' receptions). They attacked the guards as soon as they got out of the cars, but in the attack plans they had forgotten to include the nearby Café Palacio bar, where soldiers from the garrison would often eat and drink, and these now formed a devastating surprise rear guard. That was when the rest of the cars arrived. All the attackers carried only handguns. The van of the Fast Delivery Dry Cleaners, full of rifles and submachine guns, remained parked on a side street, waiting for the support group—which never arrived. Furthermore, those in charge of taking the roof of the Fine Arts Building, right across the street, in order to neutralize from there the machine guns of the palace roof, failed to do so or came too late. Nevertheless many attackers managed to penetrate the palace and some got up to the top floors—to find that the map of the building that they had studied and even memorized did not include the changes made by the dictator, among them a secret elevator which went from his offices to the roof, where he had built an apparently impregnable refuge.

Two of the attackers forced their way through by gunfire (because also, the grenades, evidently obsolete, did not explode, and rolled inertly like stones on the floors and the stairways) to the presidential offices, which were empty, of course. Just at that moment the phone rang. One of the attackers picked up the receiver and heard a voice in bad Spanish which said that it was calling from New York: a woman journalist asking if it was true that they had attacked the presidential palace. The assailant said it was true: the palace had been attacked. The woman journalist asked if the president was dead or alive. The assailant said: "The tyrant is dead," and hung up. That political lie constituted his last words: as he left the office a soldier, firing from the other end of the palace, killed him.

The only thing left for the remaining attackers to do was to get out of that building, which had become a trap, if they could. It was of course more difficult to abandon the presidential palace than to attack it and much more difficult than planning the operation, so successful on paper, so disastrous in its execution. The political group that had conceived it, the second echelon of the clandestine opposition, lost ninety percent of its men in the attack. But one could say that in the beauty of the gesture, destiny had brought together heroism and failure.

HE CAME WITH THE OTHERS, in single file, through the entranceway, flanked by policemen with long weapons. That's how they left the prison; one by one they climbed into the vans and were taken to the courthouse, escorted by three patrol cars.

They entered the Palace of Justice, where in spots you could see the old stone, which the rain, and not time or man, had stripped of its yellow lime and plaster. Some wore dark glasses and were blind for a moment in the dark interior, which contrasted with the violent light outside. Footsteps could be heard in the trial room. Relatives and lawyers and newspapermen and curious bystanders were standing around.

When going from the corridor to the courtyard where, during recesses, people would stand around talking, the line of prisoners (dressed in the twill prison uniform: blue pants and blue jacket and blue cap, which they now held in their hands) turned to the left to gather in the waiting room and it was then that the thin, pale boy without glasses left the line, stepping to one side, and entered one of the empty rooms. He hid behind the door and waited. When they had all passed by, he took off his jacket and beneath it was a shirt with red and green palm trees in a white landscape (or the other way around), which he pulled out to cover part of his prison pants. He threw the jacket and cap in a corner and put on sunglasses. Calmly he crossed the courtyard, went out on the street through the main door, hailed a taxi—and left.

The next day the newspapers published photographs

of the jacket and the cap, now black or gray, and a sketch of the supposed route of the fugitive from justice, more like a blueprint of a labyrinth. In fact, the idea had come to the pale young man that morning. He had wanted to put it into practice immediately and there was in its simplicity a charming touch of luck which made it a success. But there was no master plan, no escape maps or plots, and it was just as easy as that.

LATE AT NIGHT, milk trucks travel throughout the city. At dawn it seems that the streets, the city, belong to them. They cross the avenues and the side streets at the same speed, without stopping and often without their lights on. But one of them is not a milk truck. Perhaps it's the most cautious one, going slowly, with lights on, and making signals at each side street. Perhaps it's that one, drawn by a horse, which crosses the city from twelve to six. Nobody knows a thing. They all talk about the milk truck, but nobody knows for sure. They say it comes out of the cellar of a police station and carries inside a corpse—or two or three; whatever's around. The corpse is always a former prisoner of the opposition and if he was lucky they killed him right away. Others are tortured first, and their relatives have a hard time trying to recognize them at the morgue.

THE PLANES DROPPED BOMBS ALL MORNING. One bomb fell on a hovel and killed a family, another fell on the hospital, which had already been evacuated. The shelters withstood it, but after the attack they were full of dirt, pieces of wood and rubbish. The term "air raid shelter" suggests the military stability of a bunker or the civil security of a cellar or the subway, but these shelters were primitive and brought to mind something more like a cross between a cave and a log cabin. They were constructed in a gulch or in dry riverbeds, or sometimes beside a hill, and the roof was made of thick wooden piles tied with rope or rattan, and lastly, everything was covered with dirt and stones, and if possible, mud. They were, all in all, good shelter against shrapnel and if they didn't receive a direct hit they could be considered secure—though few air raid shelters were protection against direct impact.

There were dead and wounded rebels. Among the wounded was a communications sergeant, a blond boy with a sparse beard who looked like a peasant. He had remained behind to establish contact with command headquarters, and a bomb exploded nearby. He was wounded in the side and as the wound was small, the doctor decided to attend to it last. But now he was on the ground, holding the wound with his hands and screaming, howling with pain. The comandante heard him and came quickly. He stooped over the wounded man and said, between his teeth: Goddamn it, what kind of a man are you? Take it like a man, it's nothing, he said, and he took the boy's hand away from his stomach, looked at the wound and appraised it, clicking his tongue. Shit, that's only a scratch, he said, and you're scaring the wounded civilians. Goddamn it, don't forget that you're a soldier! he said, and got up and walked away. The boy bit his tongue, his lips, and saliva ran down one side of his mouth. He didn't say anything; he couldn't speak. He dug his hands into the earth, sinking his fingers in the grass, in the dirt. When the comandante had spoken to him, he was red in the face; now he was very pale.

When the doctor came, he was dying. The doctor called to the comandante but it was useless, because he had gone into a coma and his agony was very brief. The doctor turned over the corpse and saw that the wound had no exit, and so he decided to do an autopsy. The comandante helped him. The blood could barely be seen inside the viscera and the doctor took out a fistful of feces and among them, shining in the sun, six, ten, twelve sharp gray little pieces of shrapnel: a splinter had hit him, splitting up in the intestinal cavity as it entered, forming a shower of swift razors which perforated his intestines and burst his liver. Technically he was dead from the start, the doctor said.

The comandante wiped the blood off his hands with a rag, which he threw away. He took off his beret and walked to the radio post under the tree, and when he got there he kicked the tree.

HE CAME WALKING DOWN THE SIDEWALK, going right past the police colonel's mansion, and he entered the house next door, still carrying his package. When he was in the room he gave the package to his host and said to him: "Here's the dynamite. Put it in a safe place—and be careful, it might give you a headache. My head is splitting right now." His host brought him an aspirin and finally the young terrorist lay down on his bed in the room where he'd been hiding for six months now. They put the dynamite in a closet in the room where his parents and his eldest daughter slept. About an hour later, the other terrorist came to call for the borrowed dynamite. He was very nervous and when he left the house he hesitated a moment before going out on the sidewalk.

Is it true that no plow stops for a dying man? The cars passed by the whole night while the man was dying on one side of the highway. They must have taken him out of prison at midnight and killed him here. Or maybe he was dead, tortured to death, and a truck brought him at dawn and left him beside the little lake. Or they threw him, at nightfall, from a patrol car. They left him for dead but the man was still alive and was dying the whole night long.

Dawn came, as always. The moon was hidden early and Venus first became more luminous and then paler, fainter. The land breeze had stopped, but it was cooler than it had been at sunset. Several roosters crowed or one rooster crowed several times. The birds began to whistle or to chirp or to warble, without stirring from the trees. The sky became blue and then returned to violet, then purple, red, pink, and later orange and yellow and white, as the sun came up. The clouds came from the coast. Now you could smell coffee. Someone opened an iron gate. The traffic became heavier.

The body remained in the gutter until midmorning, when the coroner picked it up.

HIS SPRINGFIELD RESTS AGAINST A TREE. The other man, luckier or older, has a Garand rifle at his feet. It's midday and they're sitting under a ceiba tree, taking advantage of the shade and the breeze to complete the maneuvers. The two are bearded and long-haired, but one is wearing a palm-leaf hat and the other a baseball cap, and on both their shoulders, comandante's stars are embroidered over the red-and-black triangle. The younger one chews an extinguished cigar and looks attentively at the checkered mat before him: he seems to be studying it. The older one pulls on his dusty beard and smiles. There's a breeze now and the papers on the table rise in an attempt to fly, but their airborne rebellion is futile against the tyranny of stone paperweights. The young man is thinking perhaps about tactics—certain flank maneuvers, maybe a sudden attack. The old man seems to have faith in ambushes, in a raid guaranteed by the protection of night and surprise. Farther away, the rebels chat in the grass or clean their rifles, or sleep in the open air: it's not any business of theirs; let the comandantes decide. The two leaders are concentrating on the strategic operations board and they brood in silence. The old man takes off his hat and wipes the sweat off his forehead with his sleeve. Now it's the young man who smiles and offers a tactical solution. The old man wants to protest, but says nothing: he knows that war requires courage and also prudence.

They've been at it for an hour, an hour and a half, two hours, and nobody dares to interrupt them, because they all realize it's a historic moment. The shade of the tree has moved and the paper seems stained by the light and the shadows. The old man offers his hand, laughs, and announces, "Checkmate, pal," in a victorious voice.

THE CHAPLAIN WAS A PRIEST who came to the mountains like many other guerrilla fighters. He wasn't defrocked, but he drank. For a long time his favorite drink was the brandy Tres Medallas, advertised on radio with a jingle that ended in the words "Let Three Medals accompany you," and it was popularly known as Three Mellows. The chaplain continued drinking in the sierra and sometimes had problems, though everyone admired his courage and the way he carried his liquor.

Once they caught the leader of a group of bandidos and they sentenced him to death. The bandit said that he was Catholic and requested a priest to give him absolution. They called the chaplain, who came, stood next to the outlaw and said to him, *"Ego te absolvo in nomine Patris et Filii et Spiritus Sancti."* The bandit complained that he didn't know any foreign languages and that he wanted absolution in Spanish. The chaplain lowered and raised his head twice and said to him, "Well, my son: Let Three Medals accompany you." They all laughed, even the outlaw, who had always bragged that he never knew fear.

SOMEONE ONCE SAID that young men don't think about death.

This boy was sitting on the protruding roots of a *jagüey* and eating a mango. The juice stained his black beard and ran down his hands. He was laughing, because next to him another rebel was telling a story. The thing is, the storyteller said, the nephew was, you know, kind of dumb. But there was nobody else around to give his aunt the shot, so he had to do it. The others laughed. They knew the story but they laughed. So the nephew goes to the drugstore and comes back with the medicine and the syringe and gets it all ready so that he can give his aunt the shot, and she had to pick up her petticoats, and then he asks her, just like this, with his dumb face, Hey, Aunt, where do I put it, in the hole or in the slit?

He lurched backward, exaggerating his happiness, but really happy, with the mango pit in his mouth, squeezing the stringy flesh between his teeth. He saw the branches of the *jagüey* swaying and crossing each other in the sky, and when they moved the sun appeared and disappeared among the leaves, making the trees and the branches and the landscape white. He closed his eyes and saw red and black and red again. He laughed and heard the wind in the trees and the creaking of the branches and a bird singing—no: chirping. Maybe a Cuban cuckoo: the peasants call it that because of its sound, without knowing why, though they explain by saying that it's treacherous because it always chirps when it sees a man come near, and the peasants and other birds and the wild animals in the countryside use it as a watchbird. The rebels were using it as a sentry too.

He laughed, closing his eyes, the mango in his hand, his arms up high, covered with yellow right up to the olive green of his sleeve, stretching them out to gain his balance and maybe to stand up. He was laughing when the shot knocked him down. He never knew what killed him, a stray bullet from one of his comrades or a shot from an enemy ambush or what. He fell to one side and rolled from the tree down toward the ravine. What was he thinking? Someone once said that we never know what the brave man thinks.

ALTHOUGH THE THREE OF THEM ARE LYING IN THE GRASS, it's not *Le Déjeuner sur l'Herbe*. One has a hole in his forehead, another a hole in his face, and the third a hole in his neck. The second one is face down and there's something wrong with his head; perhaps it was beaten or shot up. The third one, a shirtless mulatto, received at least ten shots in his chest and stomach. In the foreground you can see a strip of asphalt which must be the highway, and behind it a segment of beach or the coast, the sea.

They don't move because it's a photograph and because they've been dead for hours and were left there as a warning.

ANCIENT FABLES seem improbable and the moral lesson is always useless: it only happens to the animals in the fables, and the experience belongs to someone else's life. In modern fables the characters are different, and this one, told all over, features a didactic father and an empty-headed son. The father wanted to teach his son a lesson and to offer daily advice that would be prophetic: like all preachers, he aspired to become a seer. One day a friend suggested a cure and the man followed his advice.

He invited the chief of police to lunch and the guest regarded his host's request as a great joke. It was to catch the prodigal son (whose only interest was drinking and women and night life) on his rounds, accuse him of being a terrorist leader and lock him in a cell. The next morning he would certainly be, as the ads for a fashionable antacid pill said, completely cured.

The young man did not get over his amazement, nor did he get out of jail. Imprisoned at the precinct, protesting his innocence, he was left in the charge of the captain with a wink from the chief. The son and that criminally exemplary Polonius who was his father ran into a streak of bad luck: the captain went out to eat with his mistress, and that night ten political bombs exploded and the Ministry of the Interior decreed the death of one hostage per bomb: any prisoner in the first ten precincts. He was in the third or the seventh and he didn't wake up with his tongue raspy from drink nor with a hangover nor with a woman at his side: he simply didn't wake up.

The moral is that the times made the fable not only probable, but also possible.

HE HAD A MEAN, AWKWARD, and sometimes, like now, a ferocious face. They shot him under the tree. The trial lasted fifteen minutes. Charges: robbery, rape and desertion; perhaps he had also passed information to the enemy. The public prosecutor was the comandante and he trembled when he spoke, saying: This man who you see here (pointing: he left his forefinger like that the whole time of the trial) is evil and you shouldn't feel any pain for him. Pain *he* deserves, a lot of pain, the pain of death many times over. Since we can only kill him once, I ask that he be sentenced immediately and that we not waste many bullets on him. The defense lawyer (a captain, who was named against the will of the accused, who didn't want any defense, and who spoke very rapidly) said that there were no possible extenuating circumstances for the crimes imputed to and, in deed, committed by the defendant, but nevertheless he appealed to rebel justice that he be sentenced to a firing squad and not be killed with one shot in the back of the head like a mad dog he said that they should remember his courage in the past he said that the desertion had not taken place and that there was no evidence of his being an informer he said for all of which he also demanded the death sentence, but by the firing squad. They shot him right there and then, against the *arabo* tree under whose shade the trial took place: only the judges had to vacate the premises. Before dying, the outlaw asked a question. Comandante, he said, how should I stand: facing them or with my back turned? You, facing them, said the head comandante. He asked to command the firing squad but he wasn't allowed.

THE COMANDANTE WALKED DOWN THE MIDDLE OF THE STREET in the dark. It hadn't rained for days, but whether or not he raised dust as he walked he didn't know, and he could barely hear the creaking of the big boots of the captain who walked invisibly beside him. They were headed for the army barracks. In guerrilla warfare a comandante has to be minister of war, master strategist, commanding officer, colonel of a small regiment, storm trooper, and even scout. Tonight he was a displaced sentinel. The regiment (or should one say the rest of them?) were surrounding the barracks and waiting for the signal to attack, a shot.

Although it was hot out, a light breeze was blowing now which moved the dust in the direction of the barracks. It was not yet nine and the town was asleep, lifeless, and if it had been another comandante, he would have thought of the ghost towns in westerns. But this comandante didn't like the movies.

They turned into the main street and almost bumped into a soldier, who automatically said halt. The comandante had his Thompson cocked. (Before continuing, it would be a good idea to give a biography of this weapon. During the early days of the struggle in the mountains, the comandante, who was not yet comandante, had won it in a battle. When he first saw it, it was traveling in a small army truck. The truck, blown sky high by a land mine, fell on top of the Thompson and it was never the same—the machine gun, not the truck. At times, when it was most needed, it refused to work. Most probably it was an excessively loyal weapon and still felt it was with the enemy.) When the comandante saw that the soldier, also ready, was about to shoot, he pulled the trigger. Nothing doing: not a shot, not a sound, not even a click. The captain realized what was happening and remembered the history of the reluctant Thompson: it's curious how many things one can think of (and do) in seconds. This man (who was carrying a shotgun, an old friend of the family, you might say: it had belonged to his grandfather, who fought in the brief second war of independence) also tried to shoot, but the shotgun copied the machine gun and jammed as if in a sympathy strike. The captain later thought that, after all, it was a weapon that had been in the house too long, employed in occasional hunting, and that it would naturally react with this untimely pacifism at the eleventh hour.

The only weapon that worked was the soldier's rifle. The comandante did what any other human being (except, maybe, General Custer) would have done. He ran; he ran as he had never run or thought he could run and he himself later told that as he ran he wondered how many records he was breaking that night. The captain, who was second in command, was now first, since he took off before his comandante. It seems that everyone ran that time, because the bullets didn't reach human flesh, and after the barracks had surrendered (the shots from the Garand were taken for the signal for the attack, which didn't last more than a half hour) they found the trembling soldier crouched behind a column in a nearby doorway, and his rifle in the middle of the dusty street.

The comandante was fair. He gave the rifle to the captain (who kept the old shotgun so that his son or grandson could hunt in peacetime, certain that there

ONLY TWO MEN came with the three hundred prisoners, the doctor and a medic, and neither was armed. They began their descent at dawn and at five in the afternoon they reached the village. Many of them were wounded and those who couldn't walk were carried in stretchers by their comrades. (In the field hospital there were still some critically wounded left.) There were soldiers and officers. The highest-ranking prisoner was a captain with a leg wound, who insisted upon walking down the mountain. The medic made him a walking stick and from afar, tall, erect, excessively proud, he looked like a field marshal with his staff. They stopped to rest at noon and the doctor and the medic handed out crackers and guava paste and water. Some soldiers helped them.

At first they had thought of sending an escort, but then they saw that there weren't enough men and they decided on this formula. One of the comandantes insisted that it was risky, that there would be a mutiny or that maybe the doctors [*sic*] would end up prisoners. None of that happened. It appeared a strange procession, the bearded soldiers (one or two; the captain and the other officers insisted upon shaving, but the troops, maybe out of laziness or a twisted sense of humor, let their beards grow) coming down the hills, with the bearded doctor in his rebel uniform and the clean-shaven medic, his long hair tied in a ponytail, also in olive green, both at the end.

They reached town, found the Red Cross people and immediately made their delivery. The army medical officers, when they arrived, saluted them, clicking their heels. They also saluted, but were too tired to click their boots together. Besides, they didn't know how to do it properly.

AT FIRST THEY DIDN'T TAKE HIM SERIOUSLY. He was the doctor, okay, but too refined, and in any case, his hands were much too delicate for war. But then, when he showed that he could go up and down the mountains like everybody else, and when he reached the mountaintop before anybody else and wasn't out of breath, and when bombs were dropping and everybody was desperately burrowing into the dirt for shelter and he continued doing a transfusion, then they began to have more respect for him and they stopped calling him Doc and instead called him Captain or (some of them) Captain, sir.

But that music he always looked for on the radio, especially at night: funeral parlor music, music for the dead. (It's also true that the radio was his and that he always lent it out and that others had it more than he.)

One day, one evening, as the sun turned pink, dark red, purple, mauve, and he left on the radio a popular tune, a cha-cha-cha or something like that, a tall, strong, Indian-looking, slow-talking rebel came over, left his rifle against the side of the hut (the battlefield hospital) and said: Hey, Doc, I didn't know you liked the hot stuff. What? he said. I didn't know, Captain, said the other, that you liked real music, the hot stuff, he said. Since you listen to that funeral music all the time. The doctor looked at him and smiled. I like *all* good music, he said. You're the one who's missing a part of the good stuff. Yeah? the other said. What d'you mean by that? Come over here whenever you can, said the doc-

tor, and listen. From then on he tried to tame the beast
inside the soldier with sonatas, concertos, symphonies,
but the music therapy didn't last long. It's difficult to
play Pygmalion in the middle of a war: a bullet or an
order can destroy the best Galatea. This rebel didn't
die; they sent him to headquarters up in the mountains
and the only music he listened to there was the song
of the mockingbird in the morning, the wind whistling
through the branches, and the screeching of the crick-
ets at night.

Every day the doctor would surprise the recruits (the
hospital was in the rear, near the boot camp) by shaving
early in the morning. He was the only officer who didn't
wear a beard. He shocked newcomers and veterans
when one day he insisted upon going to the city to
have a wisdom tooth pulled because he didn't trust
the arts of the rebel dentist. He went despite advice
and disobeyed an order from his superior. He didn't
go on the journey dressed as a peasant, because his
manners and hands would have betrayed him. He dis-
guised himself as a foreign geologist and spent hours
perfecting an imaginary accent. He reached the city
at noon and went straight to the dentist's house. Before
arriving, he slowed down and when he entered the
street he adopted incredibly extreme precautions. He
reached the door, looked at the sign and put his hand
on the knocker without knocking. He took his hand
off the knocker, went across the street, came back. He
looked once more at the name on the bronze sign and
raised his hand to his face and felt his tooth under
the skin. It doesn't hurt anymore, he said. How strange.
He made sure with his tongue that it was the bad tooth
and he was right. How strange, it's all better, he said.
It seems that the journey took the pain away. I'd better

HE'S FALLING, BEHIND THE HILL: the gray arm raised without anger against the white sky where there's a whiter sun which you now can't see, the gray hand, the dark-gray forearm, the black rifle next to, stuck to, fused with the pale-gray chest with the black stain on one side, without pain or surprise because they didn't give him time, without knowing that he's falling on the black grass, without ever knowing that they'll see him fall again and again, like this; he hasn't yet fallen but he is falling because a black shoulder, the black-gray-black pants (there's no longer any color, no olive-green uniform nor red-and-black band nor blue eyes: all hues depend on the eternal, leveling sunlight), the gray neck, the gray-gray face, the whole gray-black left side is faded, fading and vanished, leaning toward the black earth and death forever: the volley or the single shot wasn't heard but the impact is felt and he will fall as long as man exists and they will see him falling without ever falling when eyes look at him and they will not forget him as long as there is memory.

THE PHOTOGRAPH IS AN IMAGE, which doesn't always happen with photographs. The comandante is standing firmly on his two feet, in an "at ease" position. The position is military, but also Cuban and very personal, with the legs wide apart, and the breeze rippling his wide pants. His hands rest one on top of the other over the mouth of his rifle: a Garand, or a Springfield, or maybe an old Spanish Mauser. That war had been fought with all available weapons, some unconventional, perhaps even prohibited by the Geneva Convention: bamboo cannons, oil-barrel mines and shotguns filled with pebbles. The comandante's usual cowboy boots can't be seen. Behind him are some bushes that look like *vicarias*, very pleasant and serene garden plants which you often see in country cemeteries. But he's not in the cemetery because the comandante liked living things. Behind the *vicarias* there's a wooden house. You can't see any doors or windows, just rustic boards: it's a house in a country town or in the suburbs. The comandante wears an old, worn, open shirt, without a tie, with a band on his left arm which says "2 of Ju——" and you can't read anything further. From his neck hangs a striped scarf that falls over his chest. He sports the famous beard and long hair and a Texan felt hat which he always wore tipped back. His mouth is serious, but by his eyes you can see he's amused by the picture-taking and by the faces of those looking at it—even those reading this inventory. His outfit is completed by a wide belt (with a large, square metal buckle), from which a sheathed hunter's knife hangs, along with two cartridge clips, for his pistol on the left and the Browning in its holster on the right. The large pockets of his combat pants are full, as always, of grenades, pencil butts, pieces of paper, and candy, in that order. Behind, over his head, like an irreverent halo, there's an inscription (in pencil, probably on the original of this photo, this being a copy) written in wild letters, saying: "Cheo Prado Photos." Since Cheo Prado revealed his genius as a photographer here and didn't want to remain anonymous (Cheo Prado is an artist and not a scientist: more Cartier-Bresson than Niepce), his name should be repeated now.

The comandante is dead today and the same short-comings and virtues that transformed him, in six months, from a master shopkeeper to a warrior and an expert in guerrilla warfare and a strategist, also killed him, in his full glory, like the ancient heroes. In the photo you can see his gallantry, his courage, his poise, his unlimited confidence in himself, his disbelief of death, and at the same time you can see that within him there was always a skirt-chaser and a joker and an almost frivolous young fellow, who in other times and in another country would have been a bullfighter scarred with wounds, a fast-moving racing-car driver or a happy-go-lucky playboy. Because of all that, this is not a photograph, but rather that *rara avis:* the image of the dead hero when alive.

WHEN HE WAS A WAITER he'd keep a gun in his locker in case some big shot from the regime (those were his words), or secret service colonel or cabinet minister would come there to eat. Later he participated in the attack on a radio station the day they stormed the presidential palace. His cousin was with him. They survived the raid and were hiding together for a few days. Then they separated and he went to hide in the more dangerous place, while his cousin went to take refuge in a secure apartment. As one of the many ironies of guerrilla warfare, the secure place was raided by the police and they killed his cousin, while he lived to see the revolution triumph. They made him comandante, but having nothing to do, he got bored and collected weapons and ammunition in his house. One day he had a fight with his wife and set their double bed, under which he'd been keeping the ammunition, on fire. The explosions drew the attention of half the city and when he came out of the smoke, laughing, they detained him and stripped him of his rank. He was in prison for some time but then they let him go, eventually restored him to the rank of captain, and assigned him to the Ministry of the Interior, in charge of interrogating political prisoners.

A bachelor again, he now lived in a requisitioned house, or rather mansion, where he had a grand piano in the living room and a carpeted, cushioned room in the back for listening to and making music, since he was an amateur percussionist and played the drums very well. He also had a vast wardrobe (he'd change shirts several times in one night) and a collection of expensive cameras. He was always surrounded by a gang of people, and with his lean physique he looked like a bullfighter. Sometimes he had parties in his house, drinking with his friends and listening to jazz records and making music. These parties lasted from midnight till four or five in the morning, when he'd go off to do his interrogation work. There was a method to his work. He would invariably take off his shirt to interrogate his prisoner and as the morning progressed and the heat of the cell made him sweat, he'd rub his armpits and make little balls with the sweat and dirt from his armpit. Then he'd throw these vile balls like bullets at the prisoner's face. He was considered an excellent interrogator, so much so that in a few months' time he again became comandante.

THE HOUSEWIVES CAME OUT, beating their pots and pans and shouting: "We want food!" The demonstration marched toward the center of town, toward the square where "the national flag had first been unfurled."

Twenty miles from there, in the provincial capital, the captain of the garrison, who was at the same time the governor of the province, ordered the tanks to advance upon the town.

It all ended in their surreptitiously sending food to the mutinous town, while the fearless officer who had confronted pots with tanks was sent as ambassador to a North African country—and since then he's been known as the Tinhorn Rommel.

THE COMANDANTE GAVE HIM A STORY TO READ. In it a man would go into the bathroom and spend hours locked inside. The wife worried about what her husband was doing in the bathroom for such a long time. One day she decided to find out. She climbed out the window and walked along the narrow ledge that went around the house. She slid up to the bathroom window and looked in. What she saw stunned her: her husband was sitting on the toilet and had a revolver in his hand with the barrel in his mouth. From time to time he took the barrel of the gun out of his mouth to lick it slowly like a lollipop.

He read the story and gave it back to its author without further comment or perhaps with an offhand comment. What makes the story particularly moving is the fact that its author, the comandante, committed suicide seven years later by shooting himself in the head. So as not to wake his wife, he wrapped the gun in a towel.

TOWARD THE END OF DECEMBER 1958 he had embarked from a port in Florida with a cargo of smuggled weapons. But the boat met up with a northwester when crossing the strait and they lost their way. It was found, adrift, a week later, in January 1959. Fear of the sea or of death had made him turn gray overnight, and what is almost worse, delivery of the cargo would have been a poor anticlimax to his adventures: the dictatorship had fallen six days before.

In 1960 he was in an uprising against the government in the hills of Escambray, but he was captured by a squad of the so-called Combat Patrol Against Bandits, summarily tried and shot within twenty-four hours. His hair was still white.

IT ALL BEGAN WHEN AN AMERICAN went out on the balcony of his hotel the day they attacked the presidential palace and a nervous soldier fired on him and killed him. His best friend swore that he would avenge that death and came to the island and became a guerrilla fighter, eventually receiving the rank of comandante. Afterward, in peacetime, he became an expert at breeding bullfrogs. He got to breed the largest frogs on the island and this American was proud of his ability to breed bullfrogs.

But one day they stopped a truck that was carrying weapons for the counterrevolutionaries in the mountains near the bullfrog farm. This American was driving the truck. He was summarily tried and shot at 7 P.M. one day in 1961—barely five years after they had killed his friend.

AMONG THE COUNTERREVOLUTIONARIES who had just landed there was a black man. The Combat Patrol Against Bandits surrounded them as soon as they landed, and when the captain saw him, he shouted: You shit! and killed him right then and there. The other counterrevolutionaries were taken to the capital and put on trial, some being condemned to death, others receiving sentences of thirty, twenty and fifteen years of prison. But they killed the black man right then and there.

THERE ARE MANY STORIES ABOUT FUGITIVES. Many are horrible, others are unavoidably funny, like the one about the Chinaman who escapes in a washtub and is received by the exiles with cheers, but the Chinaman is reluctant to be considered a hero, repeating again and again: "Rook! Heelo's de uddel one," until they finally see the other Chinaman entering the bay, seated in a chamber pot. But the truth is not a joke.

The truth is that between seven and ten thousand persons have died trying to escape. Some have been shot down by the guns on shore or by coast guard boats, others have been shipwrecked or drowned, many others have been eaten by sharks and many more dragged by the Gulf Stream until they've been wrecked in the middle of the ocean or annihilated by the rigors of nature, which doesn't differentiate between a good and a bad cause.

WE LEFT FROM A PLACE ON SANTE FE BEACH. In a raft made of planks and car tires. I remember that in the midst of the uncertainty when we left, the doctor's mother took a little dog with her and it started to bark. It's as if I can now see them all again at the moment we left the shore. She was the liveliest of all, at the same time trying to keep the dog quiet. We all picked and occupied a place in the raft. And we took off, since it was a good, moonless night. For food we brought along some cans of condensed milk, getting which had been harder than making the raft, and also water and crackers. That's all.

Yesterday I was asked if I believed in God. I'm going to tell you something. I had been missing something in my life and that something I think I've achieved with this great proof God has given me by letting me live to tell the world about the voyage we had to endure in the midst of a burning sun and that black sea.

The days passed and as they passed our raft started to fall apart. How far we were from knowing what its end would be! A mere sign from a boat or a plane would have told us that we had been spotted. . . . An uneasiness began to take hold of us all. We had to restrict the intake of food and water. . . . Still there were hopes. But the days kept passing, increasing everyone's desperation even more. . . . And then came the moment we had all feared so much: the raft broke. Before, during the day, when it wasn't the sun it was the waves, which made us grab onto the raft so as not to fall overboard. . . . At night the cold had made us cuddle up against each other and put on the dryest clothes we had. . . . When the raft came apart each one grabbed a tire or one of the planks. Whatever we could. We had to cling to something to survive. . . .

The rest of the group had been separated from us by the waves. During the first moments we saw them at a distance. Night closed in on us. Our small group tried to close the circle as much as possible, using the remains of the raft and the rest of the tires. When dawn came we were surrounded almost immediately by a thick fog. . . . You couldn't see anything. Suddenly I felt someone pulling hard on my clothes. It was the doctor, saying: "I think my time has come. . . . I can't get up any more strength. . . . I'm sinking minute by minute. . . . I try to hold on but I have no strength. . . . I only ask you one favor: save my mother, save her. . . . Please God . . . save her . . . save her," and the doctor began to disappear little by little in the midst of that gentle fog.

Then I saw that the days and the nights were passing and I was still alive, drinking sea water and putting my head in the water, as long as I could, to refresh my burning face . . . But I was sure that I wasn't going to perish. . . . It was like the end of a novel, horrible. Someone had to remain behind to tell the story. And I got it into my head that that someone was me. That idea accompanied me the rest of those days in which I had to stay in the sea, until an American fisherman picked me up. . . . How did he do it? I can't explain. I was unconscious and the only thing I remember is that I think I asked the fisherman not to take me back to the island. . . . What I do remember perfectly is that when I was the last one left I grabbed one of the tires and put it around me to cover my backside, where I had received several fish bites, the kind of fish that can sniff blood. They did something similar to my thighs. See?

WHEN THE PLANE LANDED three thousand miles and eight hours later, a semifrozen ball fell from between the wheels. He was the lucky stowaway. The red light that had lit up on the landing gear controls was the unlucky stowaway, and he was killed falling into the sea or on some deserted part of the island that they both had wanted to leave at all costs.

FIRST THEY TOOK MY LITTLE THEATER AWAY FROM ME. You know, I had paid for it in installments with my typist's salary from the railroad. They took it away. I arrived when they had already put the requisition stamp on the door and they didn't even let me take out my personal belongings. And for what? For nothing. Because they didn't even open it to the public anymore. They simply took it away when nationalization came along and they closed it and left it like that, to rot. That's when I decided to leave the country. I requested a visa and from the very first paper, the first form I filled out, they took away my job and sent me to a labor camp. I was there a year and a half and the reason I didn't stay longer was that I got sick. I got an infection in my leg which spread from my thigh to my ankle. This I got from sleeping on the floor. They'd wake us up at the crack of dawn and take us to a nearby field to cut sugar cane and then a little farther away to plant arum and eucalyptus trees. And we were in the fields until nightfall, when we'd return to the sheds and collapse on the floor, and there would be times when we'd have to push the rats aside to make a place. I don't know what those rats did inside the sheds, because there was more to eat outside on the ground than inside there. We got so hungry that the other prisoners began to hunt lizards and birds for survival. But I couldn't do that. They even killed a Cuban cuckoo and ate it raw, almost with its feathers on. But I could never kill a bird or a lizard to eat and I got very weak working there. That's what saved me. From being so poorly fed I got that infection and the camp bosses decided to send me home for fear that the other prisoners would catch it.

I CAN'T WRITE. . . . My God, I'm a total wreck. Maybe later. Tell them that this is a suffering I have to bear, but what they've done to him is beyond words. I'm telling you . . . the day before yesterday when we went to the cemetery we were followed by patrol cars and all, can you imagine, we were quiet and respectful and almost three hundred soldiers and two hundred patrol cars blocked our way—just think, even after death they're afraid of him. Go tell the free world, if such a thing exists—because nothing exists! Can you imagine . . . I called and told them my son was dying for his country; some country—shit! Where are those human rights they're all talking about? The most terrible thing, that's what they did! Can you imagine, they bury him and three days later they come to tell me. . . . No, I'm sorry, no, no, *no, no, no!* There are no words for what they've done! I fought for twelve years to save my son and he died like a dog, I didn't even know where he was . . . they didn't even want to tell me where he was, where he was buried. Did you know that I was in prison . . . eight hours, when they finally told me: Your son is dead, we've already buried him, and I was in prison, they had me there. . . . They did horrible things to me, those bastards. This is the life . . . this is the freedom we have in this country. . . . Not a single voice was raised, nothing was said, nobody said a thing to get them to give him medical care— shit—which nobody should be deprived of. . . . Oh, yes, they all knew! . . . But nobody did anything! Even the Pope . . . What good has it done me to be such a good Catholic? . . . And to have such a noble son as he was, because never has there been a Cuban, the God's honest truth, who has sacrificed himself for this country so that . . . What they've done to him is beyond words. . . . Can you imagine, after burying him they had me going around in a hundred circles before they told me. I didn't think they were such cowards . . . because these thugs are cowards! . . . The most cowardly thing there ever was . . . You know that the day before yesterday me and twelve other women went to bring wreaths . . . and from behind the tombstones a mob of over three hundred thugs jumped out on us. . . . You should only know what it is to be a desperate mother like me, alone in this shitty world, where nobody listens to me. . . . I got tired of phoning and telling the whole world: For the sake of humanity, do something! . . . But nobody . . . Where? Here or there? Because they told me he didn't get medical care. . . . And like a dog I was, climbing up those steps of the Castillo del Príncipe. Those bastards, it shouldn't happen to anyone. . . . I was in prison even. . . . They brought three doctors to me after they killed my son . . . because what they put me through was terrible. . . . They even beat me, those bastards! There are no words for our suffering. . . . What a man he was! Ay, I don't think they did anything for my poor son there. Forty-five days without medical care! They set the mattresses, the beds, on fire, his fellow prisoners set everything on fire crying for help—shit—and nobody brought help. . . . Oh . . . they know that, do they? Some great organizations . . . the Red Cross, you say? But did they do anything? He died like a man! He died for Cuba! He died for his fellow prisoners! . . . Something nobody ever does for them—because this is the greatest loss I've ever had—they should say Mass for him . . . they should let the world know what this is. . . . Do you know what it is to deny a mother her own son's body? . . . Do you know what it is not to know how he died. . . . You know how they persecute people. I went to bring him flowers. When I did, a mob of like two hundred thugs came after me. They didn't do anything. They didn't move an inch. They came here looking for me. I had to throw them out of this house. . . . I'm demanding a firing squad, I am— let them take me to the wall. They've killed my son! I'm telling you, they took him away from me. . . . They've killed him, my son . . . they've killed him. . . . Ay, that man was an example to the world. And I don't even know how my son died. . . . Can you imagine that yesterday, the day before yesterday, me and twelve women, sad women, relatives of the prisoners. . . . Because they didn't give him up out of fear, because they were afraid the people would rise up. They didn't give him up out of fear, because they were afraid of him even after he was dead. Because I want you to know . . . the order was from higher up. . . . The order was that he had to be eliminated. There was nothing to be done! Nothing to be done! People have to speak up, they have to make those Human Rights people see that many prisoners are still walled up, they have to see what they can do for them— shit. . . . Because they're dying—shit! Shit—because they're dying! They have to make a move on that issue, you know, because there are many here. . . . I'm going to keep fighting! Because those prisoners were his brothers. . . . Thank you very much, but please do it for those who are still there, because he died for his fellow prisoners. . . . Human Rights . . . that Interna-

tional Red Cross . . . that OAS . . . those figureheads
. . . While these poor people are dying like flies in
the prisons, those bastards! You should see what the
Boniato prison's like! . . . You should see how they look
when they come out of there. . . . And I'll stay here,
I won't move from here because they're fighting, the
same as my son. . . . No, my other son doesn't need
me. He should be happy not to be here, because he
would have been in prison already. . . . No, no, impossible, they didn't let me take any calls. . . . I don't
even know how you got through. Up until now they
haven't said anything about him being dead and it's
already been eight days. . . . Tell them that he died
like a man . . . because he died for his brothers who
are in prison and he died for this Cuba—shit! Yes . . .
go to Mass . . . tell them to say Mass and to keep talking
and talking and fighting for those who are still here,
because there are still thousands of prisoners here. . . .
Now they've toned it down a bit because a real man
has died, but in a little while they'll be back at it again.
They're dying walled up in Boniato—shit—and nobody's doing nothing for them. Nothing . . . I'm telling
you, I'll still be here right with them, to die beside
them and to be reunited with my son again. . . . And
what goes on here are people who come to spy on
me and watch me and when it's not a patrol car it's
something else. That night over eight patrol cars came
when I didn't have my poor son at my side. . . . The
next day they informed me that my son was dead, those
bastards. What can you do if that thug's the biggest
murderer Cuba has ever had? Tell them that I'll die
right here . . . with the prisoners. . . . When they told
me: Pedro Luis Boitel is buried, he's already buried
. . . To say that to a mother . . . And they took me

AND IT WILL ALWAYS BE THERE. As someone once said, that long, sad, unfortunate island will be there after the last Indian and after the last Spaniard and after the last African and after the last American and after the last of the Cubans, surviving all disasters, eternally washed over by the Gulf Stream: beautiful and green, undying, eternal.

INDEX OF FIRST LINES

144